THE FOREST

Phoenix·Poets

A SERIES EDITED BY ALAN SHAPIRO

THE FOREST

Susan Stewart

THE UNIVERSITY OF CHICAGO PRESS   *Chicago and London*

Susan Stewart is professor of English at Temple University. She is the author of two previous books of poetry, *The Hive* (1987) and *Yellow Star and Ice* (1981). Her critical writings include *Crimes of Writing* (1994), *On Longing* (1984), and *Nonsense* (1979).

The University of Chicago Press, Chicago 60637
The University of Chicago Press, Ltd., London
© 1995 by The University of Chicago
All rights reserved. Published 1995
Printed in the United States of America
04 03 02 01 00 99 98 97 96 95   1 2 3 4 5

ISBN: 0-226-77409-0 (cloth)
ISBN: 0-226-77410-4 (paper)

Library of Congress Cataloging-in-Publication Data
Stewart, Susan.
    The forest / Susan Stewart.
        p. cm. — (Phoenix poets)
    I. Title. II. Series.
PS3569.T474F67 1995
811'.54—dc20   95-5774
                                                      CIP

Cover photograph: Detail of the mixed media installation *I Believe It Is an Image of the Other,* 1991–1992, by Gary Hill. Photo: Mark McLoughlin, courtesy Donald Young Gallery, Seattle.

♾ The paper used in this publication meets the minimum requirements of the American National Standard for Information Sciences—Permanence of Paper for Printed Library Materials, ANSI Z39.48-1984.

Contents

Acknowledgments

Many of the poems in this volume were published in substantially different form when they first appeared in the following publications.

American Poetry Review: "May 1988," "Slaughter," "The Desert 1990–1993"
Colorado Review: "Medusa Anthology," "Nervous System"
Denver Quarterly: "Lamentations"
Gettysburg Review: "The Spell." Reprinted here by permission of the editors.
Michigan Quarterly Review XXVII, no. 2 (Spring 1988): "The Arbor 1937"
TriQuarterly (a publication of Northwestern University): "The Forest," "The Meadow"
Virginia Quarterly Review: "1931," "1936," "The Coincidence 1956"

"The Gypsy 1946" originally appeared in *New American Poets of the 90's,* ed. Jack Myers. Boston: David Godine, 1991.

My drafting of *The Forest* was aided greatly by a grant from the National Endowment for the Arts. I am deeply grateful to Eleanor Wilner, Philip Booth, Allen Grossman, Alan Shapiro, and an anonymous reader at the University of Chicago Press for their advice and suggestions as I completed this manuscript.

I Phantom

"What haunts are not the dead
but the gaps left within us
by the secrets of others."
So says the book
of the phantom where I read
the fable of the mother's arms,
the look behind a fret of limbs,
how dread and hope are wound.
The voice fell back and back
and down, back to its source
beneath the ground.
Tell me, lonely singer, then
why the phantom fades again
there on the threshold
of our seeing.

The Forest

You should lie down now and remember the forest,
for it is disappearing—
no, the truth is it is gone now
and so what details you can bring back
might have a kind of life.

Not the one you had hoped for, but a life
—you should lie down now and remember the forest—
nonetheless, you might call it "in the forest,"
no the truth is, it is gone now,
starting somewhere near the beginning, that edge,

Or instead the first layer, the place you remember
(not the one you had hoped for, but a life)
as if it were firm, underfoot, for that place is a sea,
nonetheless, you might call it "in the forest,"
which we can never drift above, we were there or we were not,

No surface, skimming. And blank in life, too,
or instead the first layer, the place you remember,
as layers fold in time, black humus there,
as if it were firm, underfoot, for that place is a sea,
like a light left hand descending, always on the same keys.

The flecked birds of the forest sing behind and before
no surface, skimming. And blank in life, too,
sing without a music where there cannot be an order,
as layers fold in time, black humus there,
where wide swatches of light slice between gray trunks,

Where the air has a texture of drying moss,
the flecked birds of the forest sing behind and before:
a musk from the mushrooms and scalloped molds.
They sing without a music where there cannot be an order,
though high in the dry leaves something does fall,

Nothing comes down to us here.
Where the air has a texture of drying moss,
(in that place where I was raised) the forest was tangled,
a musk from the mushrooms and scalloped molds,
tangled with brambles, soft-starred and moving, ferns

And the marred twines of cinquefoil, false strawberry, sumac—
nothing comes down to us here,
stained. A low branch swinging above a brook
in that place where I was raised, the forest was tangled,
and a cave just the width of shoulder blades.

You can understand what I am doing when I think of the entry—
and the marred twines of cinquefoil, false strawberry, sumac—
as a kind of limit. Sometimes I imagine us walking there
(. . . pokeberry, stained. A low branch swinging above a brook)
in a place that is something like a forest.

But perhaps the other kind, where the ground is covered
(you can understand what I am doing when I think of the entry)
by pliant green needles, there below the piney fronds,
a kind of limit. Sometimes I imagine us walking there.
And quickening below lie the sharp brown blades,

The disfiguring blackness, then the bulbed phosphorescence of the roots.
But perhaps the other kind, where the ground is covered,
so strangely alike and yet singular, too, below
the pliant green needles, the piney fronds.
Once we were lost in the forest, *so strangely alike and yet singular, too,*
but the truth is, it is, lost to us now.

Slaughter

1

Remembering the shot that seemed to burst with no
rebound (early November, a time when the light
had waxed, but verged on turning back),
I asked what had happened and how it was done,
for I had been reading the same story over
and over of the breakdown in the fullness of the world.
I finally realized that what I had hidden from
in those early years was exactly the knowledge
that had disappeared behind the given-
ness of all things to us now. I had thought
that the very sound of the shot had created the silence,
the denying silence, around it. And that the lack
of an aftermath had come to stand for the loss,
the loss of anything I might have known then

They began with the tools, the good set
of knives, the curved one for skinning and the straight one
for cuts, and the whetstones, the steels, the cleavers
and bell scrapers, the saws and the hooks, the stunning
ax and the windlass. They told how God had wanted
meat and so Abraham went forth—resigned
to duty's technology; how some things must
be done when the season is upon us and
once begun, cannot be left uncompleted.
The animal should sleep, they said, and be given
only water—for three days before
the killing time. The stunning must be short,
exact—a blow or shot to the forehead at
the cross of an X between the horns and eyes.

2

Then the sticker stepped forward, "If you want my job, you must face
in the same direction as the animal and stretch its neck
as far as possible, then press with your foot against the jaw
and forelegs while you cut through the skin from the breastbone
to the throat—you'll see at last the wind-
pipe is exposed. Push with your shoe on the animal's
flank; the bleeding will flow most freely."
(In the wilderness a voice was burning
out of the thorn-struck bush and the stones.
God had in mind a supplement, turning
the scene against itself, and would make
what seemed at first beyond measure
something trivial, undone—a kind of swerve
like mercy, shielding us from closure.)

They explained the skinning must start with the head,
and that, very slowly, the knife should be traced
from the back of the poll to the nostril on the left,
just along the line of the eye. They said to skin
the side and a short distance down the neck
until the head would be up on its base at last and,
grasping the head by the lower jaw, they'd unjoint
it at the atlas, then cut, and twist, and pull until
it fell away, for good, on the ground.
Some of this had to be said with gestures,
but none interrupted or argued the order.
With the straight knife one would sever
the tendons at the hock joint. The hind
legs would hang then, dangling free.

3

The dewclaws have no purpose, but are taken
as a marker for splitting to the hock,
across the taut back of the thigh, and within
a few inches of the cod. Then the hide
must be split from the middle of the belly
without disturbing the abdomen's shell
or the pliant and thin fell membrane,
Each name was given by Adam in the garden
during the sultry, buzzing afternoons
after the world was whole. They warned me
that the blood spots must be wiped, and
wiped away, then wiped again with water and
a warm soft cloth. The person who does this task
must have a tender kind of attention

And must make sure no leaves or dust fall
into the tin tub where the water swirls.
The caul fat must be taken out with care.
Next someone strong should loosen the pelvis
and the windpipe, then saw and split them each,
leaving them exposed. What meaning crucifixion
has depends on display and disappearance,
for when is the material ever more resistant
than when it is contradicted? The animal had lolled,
and slept, and grazed in its given hours, then gone
to the killing floor where time was rent by pain.
"Look to the heavens," they said, "count the stars,"
and so allayed the terror of the cry.
Behind the stone, the tomb yawned, empty.

4

Later the old ones told me how
to build the tripod from timbers and
how to stretch a gas pipe between the tendons
and the shank bones. Broom-handle sticks
are tied to the rope ends, then worked, lodged
as levers, to raise and spread the legs.
One explained how the skinning must proceed
with the hoisting, another told how to sever
and withdraw the stiffening tail. Taking turns,
they went into the beating of the hide,
the working loose of the rectum, the severing,
in the final stages, of the glossy violet liver.
"Wash the liver and hang it to cool slowly;
wash the heart—hang it by the small end, too.

Keep the fat clustered against the tongue
and hang it up to drain, and cool, and dry.
Save the rest of the fat for soap and tallow.
Wash the stomach until it's perfectly clean and
the inner surface webbed with white. When the carcass
has been split down the center of the backbone,
the two halves should be pinned with a smooth
muslin shroud. They must stay this way
until morning so that the living heat
will disperse and the fresh cuts can be
cold, and cleanly made." Out of one
being a vastness; out of one task
the division of labor; out of one shot
the myriad silence: winter's gory fruit.

5

Now let us go back to the stunning,
to the meeting of a human and animal mind, let us
go back and begin again where the function
overwhelms all hesitation and seems like
an act of nature. But they were tired and had no time
for me; the immense weight of memory dragged up
and brought back into the present was, too, like a great
beast, beached and spoiled. I finally grasped
what had happened, how the real could not
be evoked except in a spell of longing for
the past or the mime that would be, after all,
another occasion for suffering.
There would be no more instruction,
no more, in the end, hand guiding the hand.

1931

Who would name a child for sorrow?
(There in Tiepolo's drawing of the Christ,
his infant hand playing in
a basin's steam.) Who, naming
the child, would give rise to this?
For the child is unacquainted,
unfamiliar, and hears
a name as just a shape, a random
softness. Who would that a sorrow
become a child, a shadow stiffening
in time? Something entered
like a mantle, a prior
contract—not burning
itself, but capable.

1936

Her mother is rolling cigars in the factory.
She is best of all, even perfect. She taps
the woody threads, immaculate, into the acrid
raw silk of the wrapping.
Best of all, she can do it without thinking or asking,
could do it while talking, but doesn't, ever.
And so she could never be the cackling
floor-boss or the foreman who stands there
tethered to the watch. She's in it, for good,
on the floor, for life, watching the strings
tucked into their casings, each brown bud
taut below her long white hands.
And just her one thought—this is my
machine—the shroud around the shadows.
You, genre painter, who finds in this beauty
and who, from this, would make an enduring thing,
or you who could build from this some plot strung
with ornaments, constructing a monument
at the site of its senselessness,
turn away, turn from the din and the dust,
and choose someone else—not her.

The Arbor 1937

A thousand bees were tensing
on the blueblack grapes and the daylight

seemed to thicken
with hum and juice and shadow.

> Coming back
> there are two there, and the little
> one can't be more than five,
>
> does all the talking, while the old woman's
> steadiness is certain.
> The air is still and hot;
> they've taken everything under the leaves.

The leaves ruffled coolly, the tendrils curled
like treble clefs.

It must have been September,
the month of her birthday. In later years
this would seem like another coming
forward into the world. But it turned then, turned
in its way from tragedy to cynicism, as if
somehow the sweetness of the dead became unbearable
and a kind of hardness would be a stay against
denial—a steadiness
that might be its own inheritance, or
just a distraction from the real—

The cushioned lid was thrown back, open-mouthed
from the basket; the clear drawers gaping

with flosses, spools, and thimbles.
The scissors had been forged

as spread-beaked storks
and were plugged by then

with crabgrass and the knotted ends
of threads.

a theatre of forgotten scenes:
on the boards small dots and crosses
that could be followed, but the point of beginning
is the difficulty.

The naked rag dolls splayed
their muslin limbs, while the newer

rubber girls lay stiffly, their blue eyes
forever snapped open.

Her grandmother had measured
each bust, waist and hips,

a ruff of pins held tightly
in her close-pursed lips.

To explain sewing, and the shell:
the point is the whole struggle
from two to three dimensions, from the mirror to the body

extended, for what is made must move with us—it is
not something entered into, but what is donned or assumed
only after a meticulous labor—
the given, her gift.

At their feet spread all the quarter-moons
of bodices, facings, and skirts—pinked

from the collars and cuffs and hems
of otherwise vanished housedresses.

A burden, for whose willing is this—
what compels us to repeat ourselves, and to repeat
what we never intended?

This is all she can remember,
and when she remembers, it is in a certain
order, but the intention
frays, at an irrecoverable edge . . .

How the old woman rose from the crackling wicker chair
and sat down on the grass with a sudden ripe weight,

her look distracted, given up, as if
another needle had been lost in the dusky shadows.

And how she leaned back all at once
heavily on the lattice, with her eyes closed,

her hands slightly open on her lap
so that the needle did slip, glinting

from her fingers, into the tangle
of grass and threads.

And then the last thing,
the part she can't forget—

the downy leaf that fell

from the grasp of the vines, a muted
green leaf exactly

the shape and size of a five-year-old's handprint

When I look for symmetry, I cannot turn to this world,
because what is known must be in movement to be true.
The metaphor is relentless, coming up with an ease

that seeks to deny every aspect of time and care
. . . handprints in plaster, the date scratched
in with a nail, the constant measurement of palm

against palm, finger to finger, an encroachment
that nevertheless accomplishes
distance. I cannot recall it, but it comes

without effort, the way the foot hits a brake
and the right arm flails out, ready, able
to save what needs saving.

as if her own hand had floated

down so softly
to land on the cheek. And how it stayed there,

unspeakable—its fall and its stopping.
How it stayed there, fast,

as if the wind had ended,
as if the sky had been emptied
of its air and its heavens;

Look to the end and
the start is gone,
to one side
and the other is lost.

how it stayed there
    until at last the parents came back at dusk, found
the two of them there,
    beneath the humming arbor.

What comes back, comes back from another
place, and doesn't save us, but alters
and, even in denying us, can turn us.

I had asked for a third term, and it came
in time, and was time in the garment
of our recognition.

The Violation 1942

Stubble in the burnt field,
her red plaid, flagging,
flagged; burnt in the straw,
stiff, stubbed,
stubbed out,
out.

The Gypsy 1946

A late afternoon in July, too early to begin
making supper, too hot to work in the garden.
A Saturday, then, and after the war, for the three
of them are there: mother, father, daughter.
But what should be clear, should be said, from the start, is that
the father always doubts, can't be sure, this is his daughter
and so has pulled back gradually to the edges
of the house, re-entering only in fury

And shame. But now he is sleeping.
Her mother and she look in the doorway
at this man, on his back, completely
clothed, against the candlewick spread.
Snoring, his mouth's precisely locked
into a wide, slightly vibrating O.
From the doorway they can see his arms
wide, his palms up, his shoes in

Opposing directions. Whose idea was it?
They say they can't remember, but one of them goes
to the sliding velvet trays of the jewel
box and untangles a green crystal earring,
then attaches it with delicate turns of the vise
to his left, slightly tufted, lobe.
The green globe dangles from its chain
to the pillow, casting a bright leafy shadow.

Next a vermilion disk for the right ear,
a white plastic bow for his hair. They think,
Johnny's not home. The room seems hotter,
more still, by now and the locusts start
to wind into a wilder cadenza.
When he stops snoring, they try to hold
their breath, but his mouth lies slack in deeper
sleep, his breathing pale and regular.

By this point they have taken out the cigar-box
cache of brushes, tubes, and puffs. They powder
his coarse cheeks, layer by layer, and draw
the faintly bruising rouge down his jaw;
they stencil the eyebrows to match the latest style—
1946, a year of constant
mild surprises. Brazenly, they flourish
the mascara's viscous wand: and then the fiery

Lipstick; what red lips
and coal-black lashes!
They discover, for the first time, they
can't look at each other . . .
. . . as dusk falls, they sit on the porch
and wait, snapping beans, shelling peas,
for supper. When he finally wakes he is hungry,
sour, and dazed a little from sleep.

He cuts everything with his fork, scrapes
his plate, without a word goes out for the night.
When he's gone the house seems to fill
with a hundred random sounds—the dishes
jarring, the tick and hum of someone's mower,
an idling car, the darning needles hovering,
some stray barks, and then a bright disk
clack-clacking on the spokes of a distant bicycle.

The mother says, "He's looking like a gypsy."
They wonder how long this spell can last—this invention
as new as a homemade fairy tale
where the father, who is always the real father,
never bothers to look in the mirror.
And those who have lived in the giant's shadow
for years find one day they
can speak, they can speak.

The Coincidence 1956

She stands at the edge of the forest.
The package she holds in her arms
Is getting heavy; you can see
She wants to give it up.

March, when the snow's petty
Retreat starts to mean
Something, at least we imagine
It so. *I cannot bear*

To remember this much
And must, then, take
Something away from the scene.

She is standing at the edge
There, where the other
Birds begin.
What is that cressy weed,

The one so blank and cheerful?
Like a serrated circle
On a lithe, clear stem—
The one that once grew

There and now, though
Nameless, grows everywhere, here.

The Spell

Stubble in the burnt field

Because my mind was tired, I fell to dreaming in the garden
and all around me flew the first last leaves of autumn.

There where I lay in the shadows, where the drowsy bees came hovering,
I dreamed of strangers walking abreast

Through the glare of a stubble field—then
a quick rush of footsteps from behind;

I dreamed of a silence commencing at the crest
of a sloping meadow, and the meadow's sheet unwinding,

And the icy fruit softened, bruised, overturned.
Adam lay i-bounden, bounden in the glade,

Then winter was upon him: a field of cold
stalks to be worked under.

her red plaid flagging, flagged

For in the midst of Paradise was the Tree of Knowledge
that was forbidden, yet the girl partook of it,

proving, in its incompletion, this was not the given
world, the finished garden that had been promised

in the closeness of the rough beasts, the shade of the Tree
of Life and Death, and the regularity of time and season.

Pain in labor was what He had intended all along;
replacing his design with her intention, her hand
        lifted beyond the picture into the ambiguous, whispering

                leaves. Later, when she cried out in the widening circles
                        before the child's head emerged, and cried again
                                as the shoulders twisted free and then

                                again at the jangling legs and slippery
                        finished base of the cord, it was the rising momentum of extending
herself that made her think again of that place.

The cold sweetness was on her lips—
        and the child's cry now across that oceanic

                space was the cry that interrupted
                        the circuit of her pleasure.

burnt in the straw, stiff, stubbed

For in the image of God, made He man.
Who sheds the blood of a human being,
by a human being His
blood shall be shed; who sheds
the blood of a human being,
His blood shall for that being
be shed. What charred the tree
charred us. Who laid a hand
on her that day
laid a hand on us.
When the forgetting
came, it came to us.
For in the image of forgetting
we made ourselves. Wherever
there was distraction, and a constant re-
arrangement of the frame,
it was the legacy meant for us.
The rain that fell in the river
was senseless, but it fell
as well to us. The sparrows
who lifted their sodden heads
and held the bits of burnt
grain in their beaks know
nothing, knew nothing, of us.
For in the image of forgetting
we saw ourselves and
called ourselves, circling,
through what we had shed.

stubbed out, out.

I thought of how in the black-and-white
films a hand with one ring smashes
the butt of the cigarette back and forth
in the plaid beanbag ashtray until
the fire is out. The tiny mummy stands
comically askew, yet is as well
a symbol of a sinister resolve.
And then I wrote down, I
wrote on the yellow paper, what
it was I had tried to remember—not because
it was the truth, for how could I ever make
my way to some place of action, cleared
of complexity or conscience?—
but so that you might
know that I wanted to know the truth
and that the truth, even without
a referent, had its own sake—
pity's sake—
the sake of pity, which can exist
even when knowledge sends only
its errant phantom,
the minister of our forgetting.

II   Cinder

We needed fire to make
the tongs and tongs to hold
us from the flame; we needed
ash to clean the cloth
and cloth to clean the ash's
stain; we needed stars
to find our way, to make
the light that blurred the stars;
we needed death to mark
an end, an end that time
in time could mend.
Born in love, the consequence—
born of love, the need.
Tell me, ravaged singer,
how the cinder bears the seed.

Holswege

I took a long walk through the chestnuts, the truth
of the light of day just above me where one wing
was replaced by another, then halted—as if a key
had been barreled over and over, to no effect or closure
in its lock. I thought of the dead ends, the little alleys
leading to the Forum, regardless of the turn

or seeming intention I might have told myself. I turned
to convince myself I meant to there beneath the fevered, true
green, wreath of the world with its glory alleluia
of chestnuts and light. It was as if I were stopped in the wing
of an endless building, a kind of ruin wound in leaves and close
by a collapsing path, the vines' creamy panicles

catching me in mid-thought with my pocketful of keys
on a rusting ring. It was always in Spring that I hoped to turn
away from myself, away from the inevitable closure
of feeling, hoping that some feeble maxim was the truth,
that what returns returns when least expected, winging
its way back through an open window, an allegory

where anyone might be the subject, if not the hero. What folly
to hope for so much. There among the keys
were keys to doors I couldn't remember. I could wring
a cloth of all its water, or complacently turn
a wheel from side to side, or try to find the truth
in a pack of cards or the crumbling leaves, close

there in the bottom of a cup. It was no use, looking for closure
before the world was ready to yield it up. Better to follow the allée
of chestnuts even if it ends in disease and extinction, the hard truth
waiting at the close of beauty. And if not beauty then the twisted keys
of what could be haltingly thought and known. This turn
to the future was of course "a kind of courage," a wing

beating forward through an overly dramatic storm. What was hard-wrung
was also comic, full of weddings and well-wrapped presents, closely
kept secrets bursting with confidence and swerving turns
of phrase—like the song that murmurs "follow, follow,"
swept up and impoverished by its own poor echoes in a key
unnecessarily sharp or flat. In truth,

there was wax, or maybe ice, weighting the wing, trash in the alley,
some blank contingency at the close of it all. Still, I rummaged for the key
to the end of the terrible sentence, a turn, a light, a face, a truth.

Nervous System

1

Aeneas stood before the pictures, transfixed, but not by love
    or self-love

so much as history—the bronze hinges crusted on bronze doors,
    the portals gouged

by war. After the wind had blown him far from fire, he woke
    in wonder, floating

from frame to frame where he traced his fame and his misery.
    Yet pity began there, too, in a mirror that couldn't improve

the story, although it could turn back time itself. Aeneas saw the end
    in her beginning and his shadowed form emerging in that place.

He knew then, not himself but how the world had known him,
    how all the while he was part of a plan, a kind of grace

descending on his fate. It was this completeness
    that now set him weeping, groaning from face

to face—hair and shoulders fading in the long drag of dust, a spear
    staggering in a senseless line. He couldn't approve

of the sailors' homesick sighs or their going from
    the battered ships, but knew that his men had spoken out of love

2

And that they would take whatever love
    had sent them. It seems that the same half-drowned
        memory now rises to the surface of our knowing. The ground

for the image is a whitewashed wall, at least one remove
    from the fullness of expression. The days fill
        with minutes; each letter and bill

slips to the floor, sealed and still.
    (I read that "deep in her veins, the wound was fed and the queen could not move
        from her frantic thought of love.")

3

Is that the one thought, the thought of finished love
   that climbs as high as a pyre of appliances soaking

outside the city limits? Like "a sketch of the modern world," the planes fly
   back and forth, the trains pull in, the smoke goes up, the subway

runs its course. The textbook explains how each second one will die,
   and one will be born, and one will need a bed;

the targets will be shifting from time to time, but the dove
   will still align herself against the chastened country and the small

cars will climb, two by two, the wavering bridge. Nature has no wit
   or symbol to console us; we saw the water fill with leaves and none of it

seemed to speak of us or draw us toward each other. Yet Aeneas knew himself
   in an image. He saw there the terrible truth of the fit

of his cruel asymmetrical love. For, commissioning that knowledge, she had sent
   him toward his future and away from the very point she hoped to prove.

Eventually the two will come before a picture where the truth
   of the story will be told. And only one, exhausted, will love

and while and wonder and wait, listening, beside the gutted portal.

4

Which of us, love,
    is meant to leave first, and which to follow the hearse
        through the city, which to note the chapter and verse

for the rest as if there were something to prove
    beyond these sunlit and deep-scarred rooms
        where shadow or candle strayed from sleep and then came

comely to the surface of a mirror, a silver comb entombed
    in a tangle of memory—why approve,
        reprise that long-wrought love?

5

They set before us their harsh taxonomy: true, steady,
    distant, tender, stormy, gone astray, love

made less by being in time. Each had claimed to be the other's
    half-world—paltry haven or hermitage

now bursting at the seams. We saw the garden "fill
    with leaves"; we heard "the wind rage

at the bolted door while the spray drove
    back the brackish sea." It's always the same, one goes
       and one stays, one turns his eyes

from the awful scene and meanwhile the well-meaning,
    sincere one spies

a flaw in the weaving the two of them have made. The task
    is repair, fray, tear, epitomize

what metaphor could take the place of time's erosion. The tain
    emerges, patternless, in the mirror there, hung above

the well-bound fire. Bright night, true story, far torch and door;
    neither yours nor mine, but both, and done—
       in the name of what could be said of love.

Medusa Anthology

1

Now my God in your firmament,
now the stars turn, inhuman, above
the grasses. Show me your face
in ice, in pond, in shop glass.
Out of the vacuum spun from
your boredom, and the humming,
electric, beneath the asphalt ground,
keep us from harm and breaking.

2

Now the stars turn, inhuman, above
the grasses and the filament
fades to red, going out.
Will you touch us again
with what you made and
then unmade? Undone;
still, stillness. Send us
the starry, far-seen, sign.

3

Show me your face there in ice,
in pond, and shop glass.
Beak to beak, claw to claw,
they hovered and dropped,
but only one flew away
to the lamppost: hold the mirror
steady and turn the fierceness back
to the eye from whence it came.

4

Sacks, bags, vents, packs, something;
someone's someone, outside the opera—O,
spare something, something to eat, want,
nothing, no change, have no change,
nothing now, nothing on me.
Thou munna' wan', munna' wan'
must not, must not, must—
have no change on me.

5

The only politic lies in particularity,
lies in gutter, gutted, or on the grate.
The grate rusted, warm, cold;
the cold, blue blanket, moth-
gnawed world, cobbled together on the re-
production cobblestones. (Lamp-
light, star-light, good-night,
ladies, goodly-night, 'night.)

6

Show me your face in ice and glass.
There was an enormous, dark, and many-
figured painting that appeared
when a plague cursed the city and
its kings. And we heard
a broken voice tell the story of a ship-
wreck, stuttering, "Wha-wha-
what is Hecuba to me?"

7

A blanket of blue acrylic, not like
the functions and forms of conceit.
"It was an embarrassment to the monarchy
that the government frigate *La Méduse*
was lost in 1816. The passengers
were abandoned by the crew on a make-
shift raft on which nearly all
perished." Perish, the thought, memory now

8

Receded. The history soonest forgotten.
"The masts and beams had been crudely lashed
together with ropes and belts and winches."
"Steering an erratic course off the coast
of Senegal." Let us draw our attention
to the adverb, to the precise quality
of action with which the thing is done—
and let us become the enemies of style.

9

Nothing but, or in, particularity.
The task of history as a cliché
about forgetting. Steering an erratic course,
on a makeshift raft on which nearly
all perished. Herded onto the slippery
beams, one hundred and fifty people
slipping, spilling, at once,
the raft unbalanced by the weight.

10

I will gladly pay you a nickel today
for an enormous, dark, and terrible canvas
on which you will represent yourself to me
and others who should like to know you
better. "It sunk three feet
immediately and the people were shoved
and huddled together so tightly none
could move or cry out."

11

The great roof fretted with gold,
the goodly frame bereft of terror
and fear—where were you when they
bundled the poor one away,
her brown coat, her matted hair,
collapsed on the curb: rain,
red tip, ginkgo budding out,
that day, the fire/medic truck

12

Blurting and wailing in flash and flash again?
Among the survivors was a woman
who wrote an unbearable story, telling how
they had promised to stay with
the raft and, together, pull it
to a nearby shore,
but the men in the boats soon cut
the cables, leaving the crew

13

To the currents and the winds, and the battering
noise of the waves.
In the night the sea rose and carried
many away and drowned the ones,
too, who could not move their limbs.
"The second night whoever could not
reach the center perished, often
stifled by the weight of his comrades."

14

Nothing pays that kind of money,
except, maybe, playing the numbers.
One of them is spending most of his time
trying to keep the clients on the welfare rolls;
still, the restaurant filled up before we noticed
and the atmosphere became, like, festive.
The hard ones always sing for their supper,
but a little Lord's Prayer wouldn't hurt.

15

Wait now boy, don't you cross
that street. 'Nice wedder dis
mawnin' sezee. Hopefully,
like really, he held
up his shield, stopping
the traffic in its tracks.
Some said the only cure for a stutter
was to sleep with a penny beneath your tongue.

16

O, what a rogue and peasant
slave are you. And is it not monstrous
that the function seems to serve
what is known of the forms of conceit?
Hector was the best and the dearest
of her sons, for he fired the ships
without a thought or hesitation.
By your smile, you seem to say so.

17

Say, sir, spare something, sir?
Be of service, sir, spare, something?
Spare service, sir, be something,
something spare and serviced,
sir, say something, something, sir,
say, spare sir, be spare
sir something, sir spare something,
be, say, sir, something, spare.

18

Wha-what is He-Hecuba to me?
Death had saved us from the waves
in the night, but the soldiers
and sailors drank themselves sense-
less. On the third day raging
hunger overtook the weakest wills
and some turned to the corpses for
their bread and meat and drink.

19

"Those whom death had spared, in the disastrous
night of wave and wind, threw
themselves ravenously on the dead,
with which the raft was covered,
cut them up in slices which
some even that instant devoured.
A great number of us at first
refused to touch the horrible food.

20

But at last yielding to a want
still more pressing than that of humanity,
we saw in this frightful repast
only deplorable means of prolonging existence.
Those who abstained were granted more wine.
But from the fourth day on, all
practiced cannibalism, supplementing
their ration of wine with seawater and urine."

21

On the sixth day, most, covered
with large wounds, had wholly lost
their reason. It was decided
to throw the sick into the sea.
When the *Argus* came, seven days
later, fifteen were left and
five died on shore. O, bright-
eyed looker in the peacock's tail,

22

What did you see beyond the
erasure? We shed "tears of blood,"
we "averted our eyes," we threw
the swords and sabres to
the waves—for they inspired us with
a horror that we could hardly conquer
as we pulled our faces tightly against
the scene of salt, and wreck, and drying blood.

23

What did you hear and not hear
in the night, was the moaning
the inverse of all this certainty
of number? For a witness can surely count,
remembering the look on a face, long before
the story is stitched by causality
and blame. Goodly night fretted
by fear, a story lashed together

24

By means of masts and sodden timbers.
How infinite in faculty, how like
a dream of passion, how like a painting hanging
so strangely out of fashion. Cassandra was raped
beside the altar, and Paris foiled, and Troilus
altered by love in unseemly, untimely, dress.
Why not, why not, why not, why not tender
tenderness, thus tendering something still?

25

What's Hecuba to him or he to Hecuba that he . . .
They bundled her into the fire/medic truck
while the dispatcher blurted
addresses and numbers, stuttering
blur so urgent and erratic.
During the curfew the homeless
lived beneath the trees and the soldiers
grew confused by their leafy camouflage.

26

That day, rain, ginkgo budding out,
spare something for someone to
eat. "That from her working all
his visage wan'd." And she remembered
the best and dearest of her sons
who, too, had been a coward,
strutting and bragging. When they left,
the print of their boots remained

27

And the dry space where her body had been.
A sweeter child there never was,
the sweetest flower of all our youth and still
not yet employed. And from his working
all her visage waned, and turned stone
cold while the rain erased her shape-
less, hapless shadow. Some
avert their eyes, some shed reddish tears.

28

It became the official policy
that on the first day of May, nineteen
ninety-two, all the boats would be turned
back, regardless of circumstance.
Day after day they studied
the sun, until the knowledge
of fire drew them headlong into
blackness, the blind spot hovering

29

Just above the waterline, drew
them the way a thread is drawn through
a needle, along a slight arch,
and then caught. *Ki sa*
u fè, ki sa w'ap-fè,
y-ava-neye-l,
mi wi tel im di
truut, di verité.

30

Show us your face, Lord,
like a spot on the sun
and we'll remember
how that black shape was
a projection from
our long-spent longing
for a starry sign
against our delirium.

31

Keep us from harm and breaking,
turn the eye from whence it came.
What are you doing
and what have you done?
They'll drown him, yet I
must tell them the truth—
how the beggar sleeps
beside the palace of music,

32

How the raft was set adrift from
its erratic course, how the woman
collapsed below the high window,
how the city burned and the boats
were turned away. How plain is
our faculty beside thy wrath
and thy will which thou hast
done. What can we see beyond

33

The erasure? Eyes to see, ears
to hear. Tongues to tell the difference
between syllable, tear, and pattering rain.
In action Cassandra was like an angel;
in apprehension, like a god herself,
but the words she spoke
mi wi tel im di truut
were all for nothing or less.

34

History soonest forgotten,
the starry far-seen sign still
send us. Touch us again
with what you unmade,
then made—slowly flame
the wire we've hung here,
figure a line between
the throw of sparks.

35

Cursed boat, and plague, and port,
tangled limbs between the planks,
sterile outcrop of the dead—
goodly frame bereft of theme,
crabbed notations in a book.
Keep the book from harm and breaking,
wake us now from awful sleep,
show us thy stone, thy stone made flesh.

May 1988

The layoffs and ransacked apartments, the
thrust toward the sycophant's hour, the
gone world of hope and opinion, the
delirious choice, the
anarchic old flag.

The hard life of soldiers and patrons, the
new ways of taming the poor, the
sad thoughts of civic officials, the
down-and-out dives, the
unheard reveries.

The specific ways of changing our focus, the
tawny cats that haunt every dream, the
émigrés in their sporty new cars, the
decision to stay, the
regretful paid leave.

The plain facts of deferred transformation, the
emphasis on the family and pain, the
grace notes of deliberate communion, the
small affectations, the
heart-to-heart names.

The egg that breaks on the way from the market, the
straw that breaks as it breaks down the load, the
meter that stops and the battery stalling, the
refusals of time, the
spies lost in the snow.

The last turn on the floor of that memory, the
last thought as they go toward the door, the
last things are the ones that endure, O the
hardships of war, the
distortions of shame.

As it turns out, it turns out the same, as
it turns out, the engine has stopped, as
it turns out, the occasion has ended, the
lights are turned out, the
gates opened, the rain.

Lamentations

1

How doth the city sit solitary that was full of people,
and that the steeples and minarets canopied,
and that the stone saints guarded
where the flute was heard in the dawn-light
and the cradlesong lowed at dusk,
and the marketplace full of made things,
the first fruits bending the tables
and the pledges and signatures of honor,
honored—how is she become tributary
and her people bounded by gates.
She weepeth sore in the night
and the tears are on her cheeks;
her face is shrouded in fear and
all her beauty is departed.
The guilds and the clans are gone,
gone the pity of the nurses and
teachers. The scavenger dogs
roam the fallow gardens and
run without strength
before their pursuers. How the walls
are stained with a brother's blood
and the night brings sickness to our longing.

2

The scribes have cast the blame
upon a woman, writing *her filthiness
is in her skirts* and the elders have gathered
in judgment under plane trees,
and the virgin is trodden as in a winepress
(how the crowd cries out against
the menstruous woman, and the handmaiden,
and the crone, and hoods them
with the cloud of anger
and pulls them into the waiting wagons).
The mothers of the warriors
are crowned with laurel and the fathers
of the singers are shamed in the square
and the signs are marked upon the doorposts
and the scaffolding built at the edge
of the fairground. Who will teach
the stitches and patterns? And who will
remember the spells of the clover?
And who will know the harmonies of
number, the names and accounts of the stars?
What thing shall I take to witness for thee?
What thing shall I liken unto thee?

3

I have been brought into darkness
surely against me he has turned
he hath set me in dark places
he hath hedged me about
that I cannot get out
he hath made my chain heavy
he hath closed my ways with stone
he was like a bear lying in wait
he hath pulled me to pieces
and made me desolate
that I cannot get out
he hath filled my teeth with dust
and covered me with ashes
I cried out to my rescuers
and they did not hear me
I turned away and still
I was hedged about
the daylight was taken
and the blanket was taken
and the rope and all
my childish things
I cried out with my throat
and my in-my-heart
and my Lord's Prayer and
my now I lay me down
to sleep and my health
and my hands and my
show me myself and my
secrets-and-all-my-sins
forgiven and I counted
the ones I knew and the ones
I dreamed and I measured
the grains of the wood
and the sand and measured

the shadow cast by the mirror
but the sun was remote and
cold to me. I turned away
and still I was hedged about
and anointed in fire
and ashes. I saw
the blue sheen
of the world through
the darkness—and the crust
and the stain of another.
I touched my hair to my mouth
and my arms to my legs
and my mouth to my knee.
I smelled the animal sweetness
and the dampness of leaves
beyond the wall. I heard
the murmurs of my mothers
and my brother alone in his
whimpering and I heard the strangers
whisper. But when I cried they did not
hear me and when I sang
they did not know my song
and when I spoke they did
not acknowledge me and when I left
they did not seek me out
along the cisterns and
streets of the city.
Mercy is new in the morning
they said and our god
will not stand for such
suffering—O god of mercy
and golden light.

4

How is the gold become dim
that gleamed from the dome
of the temple, how are the statues
broken from their mounts
and the fine-work ripped and spoiled,
how are the sons unskilled and
the daughters purveyors of absence.
All that once shone is gone
and all that was overflowing
emptied. The granaries and silos
lie open to the rain.
Mud and dust are the fodder
and rust grows on the sickle;
moss spreads over the well
and spiders web the troughs.
The tongue of the sucking child cleaveth
to the roof of his mouth for thirst;
their skin is withered like a stick
and they pine away, stricken,
for the fruits of the field.
The others crowd into their shadows
as they press into the shadows of the walls.

5

Remember what is come upon us.
We have drunken our water for money,
we have torn out the cresses
from their springs, and the berries
are dry on their hollow canes and
the foals stillborn out of season.
The lark has left the shearers and
the spruces and the elms now
yellow; our wood is sold
unto us and the stumps
recede across the acres.
We gat our bread with the peril of our lives
because of the sword of the wilderness;
our skin was blackened by famine
and our eyes stayed round and still.
They ravished the women and the maids
in the cities and the children
fell under the fen.
See how the crown is fallen,
fallen in the fallen leaves.
See how the crown is fallen,
the foxes walk upon it in its desolation.

The Desert   1990–1993

1

In the sense that the world is happened upon
    and noticed—just as one morning the children
        came into the garden where the sun had streamed
            through the larches: a perfect cone. They stepped
                inside and felt for edges in the air,
                    asking if they should go or stay,

As if they were the cause of what
    they had seen. They knew that to walk
        away would be to leave in mid-
            sentence, to turn from some gesture
                that seemed urgently felt, but opaque
                    as a forgotten language. They were caught

Then, between wonder and its guilt,
    the overbearing insistence of wonder
        when it seems the up-staging of joy.
            And they knew that the light would not remain
                forever, whether they stayed or turned away.
                Day after day the same thought

Of the country—the enormous effort of waste
and complicity mirrored in the old concerned
clichés. The struggle against forgetting
like a stream or hill eroding,
or a fissure spreading while
we sleep, for we imagine

The loss of nature only in terms
of the nature now lost, so far
from our imagining. When de Tocqueville
wrote his "Fifteen Days in the Desert,"
he said *the forest seemed so icy,*
the shadows so somber, the solitude

So absolute, not knowing all
we could have made by now and that
what could pass away from the earth
would be the earth itself beyond
its use. Spellbound, he thought
of the desert as a kind of *revolution*

In which the vast and granular world
was *falling* into its own full future
and he could, unwittingly, and suddenly,
be at the apex of that minute collapse.
History was not a line, but a kind
of hourglass, turned upside down,

As if to time an egg, and infinitely
reversing its own small, steady
progress (. . . *a light that was a slow*
uncovering, a cloth drawn back,
a lid before an eye—like a blessing
on the world, but who is the dreamer

To answer their question; the one who predicts
    or the one who follows? The blasted tree
        fell in the single field,
            the charred bark and the root
                lay tangled like a severed braid).
                The traveller arrived

In a landscape that until then
    he had only hoped for, something
        he could imagine when confronted
            by emptiness: here and there
                a cactus, a snake, what might be predicted—
                drawn on the shed skin

Of the world, these would admit
    a surface. He wrote *they have nothing*
        to fear from a scourge which is more formidable
        to republics than all these evils
            combined; namely, military glory . . .
                The children had stood beneath a perfect

Cone of light, which seemed a gesture
    urgently made by a speaker now far
        in the distance. All day
            the same thought returned: a desert
                filled with things beyond use
                and a will receded. Lieutenants

And lieutenants of lieutenants
    drawing a sandy line, wanting
        to be used and of use.
            A small cot beneath an enormous
                sky: indifferent, mathematical, true.
                The abandoned blocks of apartments, the rubble

Strewn like dunes across the view,
    caverns where vast
        machines have been severed—
           the leaking suitcase, the turquoise glass
           around the pull toy. It's all
                spelled out in the new edition of

"The New Dark": sensation, true
    indifference to all that could be new.
        How can particulars serve us when
           all they evoke is the identity of surface,
                the analogy of form which undermines
                    their history? The replacements arrive

On buses and carry sets of working
    papers. They intend no resemblance to the living
        or the dead, and no one can say
           what they dream. *They have nothing*
              to fear from . . . an empty country,
                but the fires burning in infinite regression,

The smoke refusing all shape and measure,
    the end of the long daylight of reason—
        all consequence as soon forgotten
           as the last moments of a revolution.
              A prophet in a frock coat gazed
                out into the desert, imagining

Stars as a system of justice,
    reciprocal, mathematical, true . . .
        That night I dreamed
           of Constantine's dream and how
              in Piero's great fresco cycle
                the Emperor's face between the white sheets

Is so absent and calm; his secretary drowsily
    listens as the flanking guards hold
        their conversation—there
            on the eve of what they picture
                will be an exhausting and cruel disaster.
                    And how the angel, like an arrow, or wildly

Plummeting bird—torqued from a sky
    so simultaneously brilliant and dark
        that it, too, seems more
            miraculous than made—spreads from the swift
                left wing a perfect net
                    of light and drapes it over the great

Red and golden cone of Constantine's
    tent. And then the two folds
        of light swell forward—one
            of this world, and one so surely
                not—toward us like a pulse, thus stopping
                    time in time . . .

To know what might
    be prevented, to see the luminous
        intervention, ephemeral
            and true as the morning
                light cast
drifting through the branches.

2

I understood that there must have been
    a light like a slow uncovering, or a cloth
        drawn back with all the pomp of a blessing.
            There must have been a lid
                long before an eye, a device for seeing
                    before there was seeing. And the way in which

It came can't be separated from what
    it is—like a matter to be worked
        through so work can begin. When a line
           recedes, it seems that time passes, regardless
               of beginning, edge, or end. And the seeming
               is like an event to us, with all

The consequence of something intended. It's just
    that the shape is prior—and not to see it
      is not a failure or collapse of
        will or faith, but a kind
          of belatedness that calls and calls
          again, for care.

In the sense that the pulse of the heart
    beats before its being, and out
      of the first layers all
        the organs will slowly form—a head,
          barely perceptible, surrounds
          the start of the brain

And a gaping hole appears before
    the hungry, speaking mouth. Below,
      at the beginning, the pointed tail
        will sway and the forty
          blocks of bone will start to turn:
            vertebrae, brain, and backbone

Curving while the sooty eyes lie open
    like coins in the ivory skull.
      Branchial arms and legs, gill-like
        projections that become the lower
          jaw, the neck and face suspended
          in the amniotic sac:

What has motion becomes
      a name in motion, growing toward
            an end it does not know.
                  Chorion and amnion,
                        placenta, cord, and rib; dermis,
                              epidermis, and the shell's

Filmy skin; sweat glands, sebaceous
      glands, and then the emergent surface—
            downy with soft hairs swimming,
                  soft hairs wavering,
                        from their follicle anchors.
                              The hands begin as shapeless paddles,

Then fingers form and nerves spark,
      stranded, stringing out into brightness;
            the cells of the eye diverge.
                  Ragged halo, chorionic villi
                        —jerk, swish, hiccup,
                              flex and flower.

The forehead grows, the vessels of blood
      thread, visible, under transparent
            skin. The nail beds rise,
                  the hands are shaped and find
                        themselves, grasping like to like.
                              The head turns, the face moves

And a gasping breath begins
      its sore, impenetrable
            singing. The hollow stalk
                  emerges, the stalk-end
                        thickens and forms a sphere, meeting
                              the skin's interior.

It turns on itself,
inward like a cup, and the base of the cup
becomes the fundus; the covering skin
becomes the retina. Inside the lens
begins to glisten. An iris
grows inward from the edges

Like a circle of reeds
leaning toward the watery
light, becoming light and darkness,
then color, shape, and motion.
And from the embryo's thin skin
a hollow forms beside the hindbrain,

Then the inner ear and the outer
ear, the hammer, anvil, and stirrup.
They bring the hard pounding
of the blood beyond touch,
to the place of beat and interval.

Now it hears and hears
itself in the pounding
of the other, and somersaults
into being; the one with the fontanel,
the waxy vernix, the matted lanugo
and its whorled tattoos.

One who is touched,
became touch and shape; who came
into the light, became light
and movement; who moved
into sound, became the speaking silence;
sent into time, became time emerging.

As the past increases, the future is diminished
and fear assumes the features of love.

The Meadow

When he returned from the meadow he said
that all the high grasses, coming almost
to his shoulders, seemed to be dead and yet
were also like wheat—brown and yellow with
a kind of weaving at the crest—and so,
too, could be something that might be gathered.
Then he began to tell me about the game
all the other children had decided
to play, how hard it had been, for some were
wild rabbits and others *young foxes*
although they seemed alike there in the lustre
cast by the brown-red sun. That day there was
no wind, at least not at first, and so he
explained that at the start he could see just
what was happening: if he could sense some
motion in the grass, and yet no wind stirred,
he could know "there was *some* form of life."
The teachers told about the tunnels where
the mice would spend November. Another
boy had found the caterpillar's *carapace*.
But he was unsure of the word: "was that it?"
he could not place it, but he pictured it
resembling a shell or shiny crust.
"The wind came up," and then it was no longer
possible to tell what was something live
and what was just the wind again—like

a hand in the long grass, he said, just as
the game was over. And then I asked him
about the charred apple tree and the starlings,
and how he avoided the thistle's needles,
and whether the old snow had stayed there long
between the timothy's shafts? (For that
is what I thought all the tall grasses must
have been.) But he said, "no, the snow had no
leaves to hold on to," as it did, of course,
when it fell in the forest that was there
in the distance. And he said that nothing
was alive now that wasn't the color
of grasses. He hadn't seen the tree or
bird or snow, was sure he hadn't seen them,
and he wondered what kind of meadow
I could be thinking of.

Notes

I have taken the part title *Phantom* from Nicolas Abraham's work on transgenerational haunting, *L'écorce et le noyeau*. The quote in the part lyric on the next page, "What haunts are not the dead but the gaps left within us by the secrets of others," is from the selection translated by Nicholas Rand, "Notes on the Phantom: A Complement to Freud's Metapsychology," *Critical Inquiry* 13, no. 2: 287–92.

"The Forest" is for Ryszard Kapuściński, who suggested to me that a time may come when no one will remember the experience of a forest. Robert Pogue Harrison, in *Forests: The Shadow of Civilization*, Chicago, 1992, writes profoundly on the meaning of forests in Western culture.

"The Spell": When I have used the word "sake," I have intended the early meaning of the word as "strife or guilt," as well as our more contemporary use, "in the name of." See *OED*.

The part title *Cinder* comes from the Anglo-Saxon poem recorded in the Exeter Book on the ruin of the city of Bath with its lines: "Thence hot streams, loosed, ran over hoar stone / unto the ring-tank . . . / It is a kingly thing . . . / . . . city . . ." See the translation under the title of "The Ruin" by Michael Alexander in *The Earliest English Poems*, London, 1966, pp. 28–29.

"Nervous System": The end rhymes of this poem are adapted from John Donne, "The Canonization."

"Medusa Anthology": This poem uses language from Gerard Manley Hopkins, "Wreck of the Deutschland," and William Shakespeare, *Hamlet* II:2. For background material, I have relied upon Dell Hymes, ed., *Pidginization and Creolization of Languages,* Cambridge, 1971, p. 296 (the translation of the lines in creole in section 29 appears in section 31: "What are you doing, what have you done, they'll drown him, but I must tell them the truth"); *Géricault.* Galeries nationales du Grand Palais, Paris, 1991; Charles Clément, *Géricault,* Paris, 1879; and Lorenz Eitner, *Géricault's "Raft of the Medusa,"* London, 1972.

"Lamentations": I have written this paraphrase from *The Old Testament,* The Bible Association of Friends in America, Philadelphia, 1831.

"The Desert": This poem includes quotations from William Wordsworth, "Ode: Intimations of Immortality from Recollections of Early Childhood"; Alexis de Tocqueville, "Quinze jours au désert," in *Correspondance et oeuvres posthumes,* ed. Gustave De Beaumont, Paris, 1866, pp. 175–258; and St. Augustine, *Confessions,* Book 11, trans. R. S. Pine-Coffin, Harmondsworth (Middlesex), 1961.